REFLECTIONS
FROM THE INCREDIBLE TRANSFORMATION

Also from A J Sheppard:

The Incredible Transformation of Gregory Todd

*The Incredible Transformation of Gregory Todd:
With Case Study Questions*

REFLECTIONS
FROM THE INCREDIBLE
TRANSFORMATION

A J SHEPPARD

First published in 2016 by A J Sheppard.
Copyright © A J Sheppard 2016

The right of A J Sheppard to be identified as the Author of the Work has been asserted by him in accordance with the Copyright, Design and Patents Act 1988.

All rights reserved.

No part of this publication may be reproduced, stored in a retrieval system or transmitted, in any form or by any means without the prior written permission of the publisher, nor be otherwise circulated in any form of binding or cover, other than that in which it is published and without a similar condition being imposed on the subsequent purchaser. The only exception to this is for brief quotations in reviews.

All Scripture quotations are taken from the Holy Bible, New International Version®, NIV®. Copyright ©1973, 1978, 1984, 2011 by Biblica, Inc.™ Used by permission of Zondervan. All rights reserved worldwide. www.zondervan.com. The "NIV" and "New International Version" are trademarks registered in the United States Patent and Trademark Office by Biblica, Inc.™

A CIP catalogue record for this title is available from the British Library.

Paperback ISBN: 978-0-9933424-2-4
Ebook ISBN: 978-0-9933424-3-1

Book cover design by Samuel Nudds Design and Vision Tank
Book design by Vision Tank

www.ajsheppard.com

For Blair McCallum

Introduction

THE inspiration for this book comes from the many parallels I have seen between lessons I have learned in business and discoveries I have made on my quest to make the most of life as a whole. For example, just as my first encounter of business transformation took me by surprise when I should have known better, so did my first significant spiritual encounter. I will say more on that later on…

Each left-hand page in this book will describe what I suggest is a business truth. The essence of this truth is then reflected to the right-hand page, where I apply it to the search for meaning and fullness in life as a whole. Each left-hand insight is developed from a quotation from *The Incredible Transformation of Gregory Todd*, the management novel I crafted to show what transformation can look like, how to achieve it and the pitfalls to avoid. Since each management insight is outlined within the corresponding reflection, it is not necessary to have read the novel first.

Today it seems that life can be more fragmented than ever. For example, business books are for business people and spiritual books are for spiritual people. This book intentionally mixes things up, because I believe this can be a helpful step towards leading a more integrated and balanced life. After all, each of us has a single mind, heart and soul with which to embrace life as a whole. Just as fragmentation can create unnecessary tension and constraints within an organisation, so I believe it can for an individual's life.

For a similar reason, during the incubation of *The Incredible Transformation of Gregory Todd*, I took the opportunity to develop the storyline as a subtle allegory for my own spiritual journey and Christian faith. It was important to make the allegory non-explicit so that the novel can still serve first as a business book. Gregory represents each of us as an individual, or sometimes mankind as a whole, and the way he runs his business represents how we might choose to run our lives. Not everyone will be interested in the deeper meaning, although I know many people who work in business and who continue to think a lot about life beyond work. If you would number yourself among such people, I hope this book will be of interest, even if you may already have formed views on the relevance of the Christian faith.

To sum up, this book can be considered as an exploration of lateral thinking between business life and spiritual life. My hope is that it will serve as a celebration of – and a guide to – life in all fullness.

A J Sheppard, May 2016

"As water reflects the face, so one's life reflects the heart."
(Proverbs 27v19)

1. Time Management

"He tried telling me to separate the important from the urgent!"
(Chapter 7, *The Incredible Transformation of Gregory Todd*)

When asked how they are, people at work often answer with one word: "Busy!" I don't think I have met many people who would describe their work otherwise. Beyond regular tasks there is always plenty more that can be done.

Under this pressure, time tends to be swallowed up by urgent matters. Days roll into weeks, and some important matters remain unaddressed that we are able to put off for a little longer. For this reason, good time management prescribes the discipline of setting aside time to address the important amid the urgent.

Two of the most important types of questions for any organisation are:
- What are we looking to accomplish as a whole?
- How well are we currently aligned to accomplish this?

The first question concerns strategy, for which most organisations do prioritise time. The second question is part implementation, part culture. In my experience many organisations do not quite seem to get around to addressing this properly. Therefore each revised strategy can be met with incredulity from a workforce who feel they are living a different reality. However, when both questions are addressed well, I have seen that it is possible for everyone to feel fulfilled and motivated to work together to accomplish the same goals.

1. Time Management

Beyond work, time can prove even more scarce and precious. For example, one colleague approaching retirement told me that his single regret was not investing more time with his children when they were younger.

In whatever time is available outside work, it is easy to live from week to week or year to year without considering some of the more important matters in life, including how we can get the most out of life as a whole. Even if we feel we are already pursuing a good course, it can still be of value to come up for air every so often to re-evaluate the bigger picture. Are the different parts of our life in balance and working towards the same goals? Do we still value the same things as when we set our course? If we are climbing a ladder, is it leaning against a meaningful wall? Is it possible there is something we are missing?

The aim of these reflections is to consider some claims which, if true, have immense personal value. In setting aside the time to explore this material, I hope you will consider it a worthwhile investment in the 'important'.

2. Being Hypothesis Driven

"Being hypothesis driven is the key to overcome inertia."
(Chapter 14)

When I started as a management consultant with McKinsey & Company I was trained to be "hypothesis driven". This means starting with a hypothesis – an educated guess – of a solution and driving towards it. For example, during my first engagement the McKinsey expert assigned me specific tasks such as to "prove that if we process parts like *this*, the entire assembly operation can fit into *that* amount of space". This initially seemed counter-intuitive and a little uncomfortable. As an engineer my preference was to work systematically *towards* a solution. Being hypothesis driven seemed like jumping to a solution too early.

The argument for a hypothesis-driven approach is to benefit from experience and to act quickly. Data in a typical business is abundant and complex: everyone has an opinion of what needs to be fixed, and sales, production and margin data can vary across thousands of products. The amount of data needed to test a hypothesis is a fraction of this. Therefore by forming a good hypothesis, inertia can be overcome by making progress towards a good solution almost immediately. The approach remains rational because each hypothesis is to be tested with relevant data and rejected or modified if the data disproves it.

I warmed to the idea of being hypothesis driven when I saw the depth of transformation it helped us to achieve so quickly. My full commitment was sealed after relying on it for engagements I went on to lead. One of my early clients summed up the benefits like this: "In four months you've helped us to transform our business. Our last consultants were in here for *six* months and they were still analysing data."

2. Being Hypothesis Driven

So how, then, can we make progress in a quest to get the most out of life? This question can, of course, provoke further questions, including whether there is purpose behind life itself. This can take us in a number of different directions, and in any of these there is probably a myriad of self-styled experts offering answers and citing evidence or data to back up their ideas. How can anyone hope to systematically analyse all of this data? Perhaps unsurprisingly, many of us give up, maybe parodying the idea of finding meaning in life, and re-immerse ourselves in getting on with life as best as we see fit.

I would like to suggest an alternative approach. This is to start with the hypothesis that there is *something* of value in the man known as Jesus.

I trust this sounds relatively reasonable. You may already know that Jesus claimed *his* purpose in life was so that people "may have life, and have it to the full". Why *not* start here? Despite humble origins and a short life, it can be argued that Jesus has influenced the world more than any other leader or teacher. These reflections invite you to test these claims, although it is highly likely that you already have some knowledge of Jesus and the religion that is now associated with him. Therefore I would like to challenge you to try to leave your existing views, motivations and associations (both good and bad) to one side for now. In doing so, I invite you to test this hypothesis afresh, with an open mind.

3. Untapped Potential

"How could he unlock this internal energy?"
(Chapter 6)

For the last sixteen years I have specialised in helping leaders to transform their operations – especially within manufacturing businesses. When I visit a factory, I have learnt to see beyond the potential for improved results, to the potential for transforming its culture. Most factories employ good people who know their work well and want to do a good job. But many do the same work day in, day out, and endure the same frustrations and problems. What if people could look forward to coming to work, where they know they can grow, contribute and have fun as they solve these problems together? What if a leader could somehow unlock this potential? Could this release a limitless source of energy from within their organisation?

Sadly, I have seen leaders try to orchestrate this kind of cultural transformation with empty talk, which can typically suppress morale even further. But as leaders address substantial issues within their organisation and engage an effective change-management vehicle, cultural transformation can indeed be precipitated. I will always remember the first time I witnessed this: there was a palpable buzz in the workforce. The workplace did not just *look* different, it also *felt* different: people were proud to be part of it. Fresh energy was being generated, and it was contagious. A clear expression of this from another early client was when someone from a relatively untouched area within the organisation came forward with a technical idea to save many times his salary in material costs. It was one of many signs that the whole organisation was bursting into life.

3. Untapped Potential

"Whoever believes in me, as Scripture has said, rivers of living water will flow from within them." (John 7v38[1])

Jesus used metaphors to paint vivid pictures of the potential he saw for us to enjoy fullness of life. For example, "rivers of living water" evokes the potential for a limitless source of life and refreshment flowing from within.

While at university I began to question how much I really knew about Jesus. I still went to church in an increasingly non-Christian country, so I found myself talking about him more than most. But while trying to explain to a friend my accepted belief that Jesus had made things of "God" available to me, I became convicted that I wasn't even convincing myself. I realised that many of Jesus' claims did not particularly resonate with me. But what if they could? What if Jesus *had* been telling the truth? In one sense I felt like I was already living life to the full: I was doing well, enjoying life and I had no needs to speak of. But if *more* was available, I wanted it. I knew Jesus taught people to talk to God and to address him as "Father", so I resolved to give this a proper try. If Jesus *had* been telling the truth, any God that existed could perhaps find a way of making himself known (together with any "more" that might be available). If not, I would live a life free of religion, making the most of it however I saw fit. Although I would not have used the term at the time, I had begun to practise a *hypothesis-driven* approach.

---

[1] The life and teachings of Jesus were recorded by eyewitnesses in the accounts of Matthew, Mark and John. These, together with the account of Luke which was developed from them, are now the first books of the Bible's New Testament. Its Old Testament contains the scriptures to which Jesus referred, which principally outline the history of the Jewish people.

4. INVESTMENT

"If you want to see a transformation, resource it."
(Chapter 9)

One of the first hurdles of facilitating transformation is persuading senior managers to invest enough time in it. Firstly, I advise leaders that they should free up enough of their own time (typically at least 20%) to lead their organisation *through* the transformation. Secondly, I ask leaders to free up some of their best managers and employees to dedicate themselves full-time to the transformation initiative. I am often challenged as to whether this is really necessary: *why can't people get transformation done through their existing roles?*

I have great empathy for leaders who baulk at the idea of freeing up anyone, let alone their best people. Of course it is not easy, but it is a question of reprioritising people for long enough to make transformation happen. Designing substantial improvement cannot be done on the side. In my experience, to successfully transform an operation of fifty to one hundred people in four to six months, a full-time team of five capable "change agents" is required, led by one expert. These change agents should represent a mix of the organisation's best people in order to embed learning from the expert, to shape better solutions and to influence others so that the new ways of working will be properly sustained and improved.

I have never known any organisation to transform just by exhorting everyone to work harder in their existing roles. I *have* repeatedly seen success where managers invest their most precious commodities of time and capability in the transformation process. Such investment in itself is evidence of prioritisation, the most critical success factor for achieving any business change.

4. INVESTMENT

"So do not worry, saying 'What shall we eat?' ... But seek first his kingdom and his righteousness, and all these things will be given to you as well."
(Matthew 6v31,33)

Jesus exhorted us to invest in *seeking* Father God as a priority. Here he associates this with a search for "righteousness": a term describing a "right" way of living that God prescribes. This suggests that if we are willing to invest in seeking God on his terms (i.e. with a willingness to change), we will find him. Elsewhere Jesus promised, "Blessed are those who hunger and thirst for righteousness, for they will be filled" (Matthew 5v6). The scriptures from which Jesus quoted also contained a similar phrase from the prophet Jeremiah, purporting to be from God himself: "You will seek me and find me when you seek me with all of your heart" (Jeremiah 29v13).

When I started talking out loud to any Father God who might exist, it felt pretty awkward – so I made sure I spoke very quietly! It would definitely have been easier not to do it, but somehow it seemed important enough to take the risk. I can't claim that investing this time in "prayer" was a strategic decision: it was more that I felt compelled to try it. I remember making use of travelling time by mumbling out thoughts to Father God instead of keeping thoughts in my head. The difference between praying in this way and thinking initially seemed superficial, but after a while I was surprised to hear what I was voicing. I was expressing hopes and fears that I had never "heard" in my mind, as if they were coming from deeper within. I still couldn't be sure that anyone was listening, but I had stumbled across a way of expressing my whole, honest self. It felt unguarded and vulnerable: my whole self was now invested in the search.

5. Listen

"Some of you may feel that we haven't listened to you well enough in the past."
(Chapter 10)

It can sometimes be dispiriting how many people volunteer negative things about their managers while I work in their organisation. One of the common complaints I hear is, "They never listen!" It is often evident through someone's expression how much this has affronted them. I also have plenty of my own examples where instead of feeling listened to I have encountered prejudice, a cold shoulder or complete misrepresentation. My most memorable example of this was when I was greeted with the words: "Go on, *you* tell me what you want to do, and *I'll* tell you why it won't work!"

But how good are *we* at listening to others? I know how easy it is to become so focused on our own agenda and consumed with our own pressures that suggestions, ideas or opinions from others can seem like interference. It is tempting and easy to dismiss them without giving them proper consideration. The stock phrase, "I hear what you're saying, but…" is often now considered a euphemism for, "I really can't be bothered with what you're saying." But beyond the need to listen in order to respect and honour people, what if someone really is issuing a warning that will avert disaster? Or what if someone's ideas could deliver more than we have ever dared to dream? We need to rediscover and embrace listening for our own benefit. This means adopting a mindset that is always open to inviting and understanding what someone has to say, and to considering its relevance and potential impact for our own situation.

5. LISTEN

"Whoever has ears, let them hear."
(Matthew 11v15)

Jesus urged people to listen to him properly and to consider his words. Many of these words were recorded by first-hand witnesses who travelled with him or who came to see him. These sayings are now included throughout the first four books in the Bible's New Testament, making the words of Jesus widely available.

In addition to talking out loud to the hypothetical Father God, I also felt I needed to listen – at least to what else Jesus had to say about him. Having considered myself to be a Christian for a while, I was already familiar with many of the things that Jesus said and did. However, my knowledge of the Bible was a bit like the knowledge of London I had gained through visiting it by train and underground: I knew how to pop up at some of the famous bits, but I had never really considered how everything was connected.

My own religious associations meant that I was slightly taken aback to discover that in a contemporary translation, the biblical accounts of Jesus' life were readable and engaging. Jesus was a more complex character than I had assumed him to be: he made many potentially inflammatory remarks, as well as his extraordinary claims. These claims supported the Christian knowledge already in my head, but they still did not seem to strike any particular chord with me. I was still unconvinced that they had much relevance for the life I was living at university in late twentieth-century Britain.

6. ALL CHANGE

"Are you effectively assuming that change is required from everyone except you?" (Chapter 13)

Most senior managers who initiate a change programme see their role as a combination of planning and directing the programme, and challenging and motivating their workforce.

While a change programme *does* require careful management in this way, I have learnt the importance of challenging leaders to see beyond this. If managers assume that their only role in change is to *manage* it, they are effectively implying that change is only required in the way that *other* people work. This can appear hypocritical to the workforce, and it can propagate a rift and a lack of trust and respect for senior management. Moreover, leaders have probably already shaped the organisation *more* than anyone else. Therefore if the organisation still needs to change significantly, there is a logical argument that the thinking and behaviour of its leaders might need to change the most.

In my experience, there are nearly always two ways in which leaders will *need* to change their thinking and behaviour to effect substantial and sustainable change. First, they will need to listen to reveal and then undo actions that may have been taken with good intentions but are having adverse consequences. Second, they need to model a good culture where people are empowered and equipped to diagnose and solve problems in the areas for which they are responsible.

6. ALL CHANGE

"How can you say to your brother, 'Let me take the speck out of your eye,' when all the time there is a plank in your own eye?" (Matthew 7v4)

While reading about Jesus, I could not escape how much he had to say about attitudes and actions that he considered outside Father God's guidelines for the good of mankind. He used the term "sin" to describe such thoughts and actions. Like most people, I had never claimed to be perfect, but it still seemed evident that the much greater problem was the sin in other people. Through constant news reports of killings, corruption and abuse it seemed evident that self-serving attitudes and actions were rife and behind many of the world's problems. In comparison, I seemed to be leading a relatively good life: surely change was mainly required of *other people*, not me? I did not see it at the time, but my views were embodying the same essence of hypocritical judgement that Jesus was criticising: it was as if my perspective had been skewed by the plank in my own eye.

Strangely, although I did not *think* I needed to change, I rediscovered within me more of the desire I had known as a child, to help others. I had sometimes exercised this through voluntary work, so I thought it might be good to do some more of this. I had an opportunity to do so in my long summer holiday, after my usual work placement for Shell, with whom I had won sponsorship. But I had already developed a pattern of using this remaining holiday to go backpacking somewhere adventurous… so I hit upon the inspired solution of pursuing voluntary work overseas! I remember asking Father God to help arrange this for me, if he was listening and able. After hearing nothing and being rejected by an overseas charity, I reverted to Plan A. That year, it would mean joining friends in Hong Kong and backpacking together around China. I'll pick up this thread again later…

7. Waste Not

"To become a world-class company, everyone should learn to see and to eliminate these types of waste." (Chapter 14)

In the early 1990s, Toyota's practices became widely recognised outside Japan as the benchmark for how best to configure and run a manufacturing facility. A quarter of a century later, Toyota's reputation in this field of operations management remains unsurpassed. How has it managed to achieve this?

In the late 1940s Toyota started to discipline itself to look *internally* for improvement potential. This became its preoccupation, rather than benchmarking itself *externally* by measuring its performance against that of other companies. It did so by focusing on reducing what it called "waste": anything it was doing which did not add value in the eyes of the customer. To teach its own people to identify and eliminate this waste, it defined seven types of waste typically seen in manufacturing businesses:
WAITING of parts for processing; or of people, for a task to perform;
INVENTORY: raw material, WIP or finished products;
MOTION within a process;
OVERPROCESSING to an unnecessarily high standard;
TRANSPORTATION between processes;
OVERPRODUCTION: producing more or sooner than is needed;
REWORK: of a product through a process, or material that has to be scrapped.

This list has helped Toyota's workforce to continuously direct its problem-solving skills to achieve more of its potential. It not only helps to paint a picture of what excellence can look like, but it also helps its workforce to work towards it.

7. WASTE NOT

"There is only One who is good. If you want to enter life, keep the commandments." (Matthew 19v17)

Jesus expanded his teaching on sin to a young man who approached him. "Teacher," he asked, "what good thing must I do to get eternal life?" (Matthew 19v16). Jesus chose to reply using the term "enter life", perhaps to emphasise the fullness of life *before* death that he was also offering. When the young man asked him to clarify which commandments he needed to obey, Jesus gave him a list of six types of sin to avoid:
"Do not murder;
Do not commit adultery;
Do not steal;
Do not lie;
Honour your father and mother;
Love your neighbour as yourself."

Whenever I came across a list like this in the Bible, my immediate response was to see how I might stack up to it compared to other people. In this way I was more concerned about external benchmarking than looking internally for my own improvement potential. Therefore when Jesus implied that *no one* except Father God was good, I found his words a little harsh and condemnatory. (At this stage I had not considered that the list could prove more helpful than a benchmarking exercise. See Reflection 25: The Freedom Paradox.)

8. SAFE AS HOUSES?

"The company needs saving, does it?"
(Chapter 13)

Every connection I make with a business starts with their desire to *improve*. I can't recall a client ever expressing a need to be *saved*: if they did, it might well be too late for the expertise I can offer. Yet it is sobering to recall corporate brands which were once household names and have since disappeared. A good business knows that if it does not keep improving, it will stagnate or decline. For this reason, helping a business to thrive can also be considered as the surest route to *saving* it from demise.

The first step in managing change is to diagnose the opportunity for improvement. The purpose here is to establish whether there is sufficient opportunity to meet the specific *need* to improve. I have only worked with one business where insufficient opportunity could be found to meet this need. (This automotive component business had requested help to improve productivity, but we established that its managers had already presided over such a demise that it could not have returned to profit, even if the entire workforce could have worked for nothing.)

In this light it should be considered good news if enough opportunity can be found early on to confirm that the desired improvement *is* possible. However, this perspective is understandably rarer among seasoned managers. Many may be offended by the suggestion that significant further potential remains, inferring that their achievements to date have not been *good enough*. Although the diagnosis process plays a vital role in helping everyone to thrive, it can appear condemnatory to those who are proud of their achievements to date. The diagnosis should therefore be led sensitively, and good interpersonal and influencing skills can be critical.

8. SAFE AS HOUSES?

"For God did not send his Son into the world to condemn the world, but to save the world through him." (John 3v17)

Jesus' words can seem inflammatory to those who are leading what they already consider to be a good life. For example, his insistence that only God is good and that no one can enter life without obeying God's commandments can seem like unnecessary, unwelcome condemnation. Yet Jesus insisted that Father God's purpose was not to condemn but to save, and that God's Son would play the critical role in this rescue. Jesus also claimed that *he* was this Son. He knew that in making these claims, he risked being charged with blasphemy by the religious authorities of his day. And so these charges were brought against him, and became the focus of his arrest, trial and crucifixion.

I was familiar with Jesus' claim that he had come to save the world. For example, in the preceding verse he said, "For God so loved the world that he gave his one and only Son, that whoever believes in him shall not perish but have eternal life." This was the type of claim I no longer seemed able to accept at face value. I was happy, enjoying life and making the most of every opportunity. With good friends, family and health, I was also far too young to be worried about death: especially because there was nothing I could do to prevent it. I felt no particular need to be saved from anything. With hindsight, I can see I was already proud of what I considered to be my own achievements in life so far. Instead, I found myself voicing a deeper hope that if Father God existed, he would consider me to be OK, or at least no worse than the majority. If there was anything beyond death, I was perhaps trusting that I would find a certain safety in numbers. I still wanted *more* from life if it was available, but I had never considered that this might be something Father God could be saving us *for*.

9. Implementation

"Analysis is fruitless until it is seen through to improvement."
(Chapter 18)

To change any organisation for the better it is, of course, not enough for people to *think* differently: people must also *act* differently. This may sound obvious, but I have seen circumstances conspire so that implementation can be readily overlooked.

I have learnt the benefit of giving just long enough for the "diagnose and design phases" (e.g. two weeks each), so implementation can begin as soon as possible. Ideally, this is just long enough to focus the cross-functional change team on grappling with new ideas, working out how they can be applied, and examining potential solutions from every angle. At the end of this intense design phase, managers are asked to present and explain their proposed solutions to their Steering Committee. Gaining agreement in this meeting can seem like a climax. I have therefore seen senior managers respond by celebrating the team's achievements and asking if they can design something similar for another area. In moments like this it can seem that everyone has forgotten that nothing has actually changed in practice!

Putting a new idea into practice can also seem like an anti-climax after the stimulation of discovering and examining it, but doing so is equally challenging. Instead of philosophical and technical insight, managers need further change-management insight. They also require great commitment to influence the hearts and minds of those involved so that the solution can be successfully owned and sustained. Leaders will need to deal with implementation barriers, and demonstrate their commitment by addressing further issues that the implementation will bring to the surface. Ultimately, the impact of any good idea can only be as good as its implementation.

9. Implementation

"But everyone who hears these words of mine and does not put them into practice is like a foolish man who built his house on sand." (Matthew 7v26)

To change our lives for the better, it is not enough for us to think differently: we must also act differently. This sounds obvious, but as someone who loves to grasp new concepts, I have become aware how prone I can be to neglect putting good ideas into practice.

When a simple idea is repeated, I can find myself thinking, "I already know that – tell me something new." With such a predisposition it is easy to become very familiar with an idea – and to approve of it as a good one – yet neglect to do it. For example, one of Jesus' most familiar teachings is, "Do to others as you would have them do to you" (Luke 6v31). I imagine that most of us know and would commend this idea, but how much effort do we invest in practising it?

Jesus reminds us that it is futile to hear any of his teaching unless we are also prepared to put it into practice. This requires insight into our own will and motivations. It also requires focus and commitment to see his teaching through to fruition. Ultimately, the fruit of Jesus' teaching can only be as good as its implementation.

10. OUT OF OUR COMFORT ZONE

"If anyone can save even another ten per cent, I'll eat my hat."
(Chapter 4)

I started learning the art of transformation within McKinsey's Production System Design Centre. This nurtured a sheltered learning environment for new consultants like me, as well as for the smaller clients it served. These "learning partners" were engaged on the basis that transformation was the agenda, rather than addressing a more specific but less holistic need. My own expectation for my first transformation had been shaped through experience I had gained in delivering improvements within Shell and Crown Cork. Privately, I was hoping we could come up with enough good ideas to yield a ten per cent improvement – or twenty if we were lucky.

Thankfully, the engagement was in the hands of an unconventional, hired-in trainer who had been shaped by entirely different experiences. I soon felt out of my comfort zone in a whirlwind of activity. Within four months we had roughly doubled productivity and capacity *and* two facilities were being consolidated into one. Everything had been achieved through the workforce who seemed as stunned as I was, yet were full of pride and further ideas. Beyond the improvement figures, the organisation's culture had transformed: it was now brimming with fresh verve.

Before this encounter I would have argued, based on my professional experience, that transformation like this would have been impossible to achieve in practice. This would have been tantamount to assuming I had already experienced nearly all there was to experience! If I had been left to my own devices, my assumption would sadly have been self-fulfilling. However much value we place in our own experience, we must stay humble enough to prevent it *limiting* our future experiences and potential.

10. OUT OF OUR COMFORT ZONE

"We testify to what we have seen, but still you people do not accept our testimony ... how then will you believe if I speak of heavenly things?"
(John 3v11-12)

I had assumed that if Father God existed and there was truth in Jesus' claims, he could find a way of letting me know. I had subconsciously assumed that I could *know* this just as I gained knowledge about most things: through books, science and/or by grappling with concepts in my mind until they made sense. With hindsight, I now see how foolish that was, and that these expectations had been shaped by my limited experience. In particular, I had spent little time considering anything beyond the natural world in which I was immersed. Consequently, I was woefully unprepared for the encounter that transformed my life.

It came one evening while I was on placement with Shell in the South of France. Alone most evenings, I had plenty of time to continue talking out quietly and reading the Bible. The trigger came when I had asked Father God to explain something (more on that later). Within minutes I was lying prostrate on the floor of my room in the presence of Father God, who had suddenly become very real. I still struggle to relate what happened in the same words I use for natural experiences. I could not stand or even kneel. My heart was being filled by wave after wave of something so powerful that I felt compelled to unburden it by going out on to the street and hugging strangers. I was relieved to find I could override this compulsion, but the waves kept coming until finally my heart could withstand no more. I was forced to cry out to Father God to ask for it to stop, and mercifully it did. I felt wrecked and wonderful. My life had changed, as had my perspective on everything.

11. Starting Afresh

"Let's start with a blank sheet of paper and imagine we're designing the operation from scratch." (Chapter 7)

In my experience, organisations give much less attention to designing their overall operations than they give to designing their products or services. Consequently, in new factories equipment is often bolted down with a good sense of overall flow but with insufficient consideration given to how lead time, productivity, inventory, customer lead times or quality will be influenced. Factories also tend to evolve as new processes or extra inventory are fitted in wherever space can be found. All of this can influence the organisation's performance and the customer's experience just as much as the design of the product.

Before designing potential changes to an operation I find it helpful to ask managers to imagine making a fresh start. I take a blank sheet of paper and lead them through a process of designing their ideal operation afresh, from scratch. We then acknowledge practical constraints (such as equipment with immovable foundations) and modify the design around these. This process always reveals how significant benefits can be achieved. However, just as change-management skills are required for the diagnosis (Reflection 8), they are equally critical for leading different people through the design phase in different ways, depending on their receptivity to making a fresh start. Some managers may jump at the chance, if for example they have been struggling daily with operational problems that they have never before felt empowered to solve. More complex influencing skills are needed to work with a manager who takes pride in how they have shaped their operation into what it is today. The difficulty of helping a manager to *realise* the available benefits tends to be proportional to the pride they have in their current operation, irrespective of the potential that still remains.

11. STARTING AFRESH

"You should not be surprised at my saying, 'You must be born again.'"
(John 3v7)

Jesus said that making a new start in life was not just a possibility but an imperative for everyone. He said that such a new start equated to being born *again*: this time by spirit rather than flesh, and initiated by the Spirit of Father God himself. Later in the New Testament this new start is equated to having our past life and mistakes buried with Jesus – and being raised to new life with him. Each new life is uniquely designed by Father God and can be lived out in partnership with him, once our relationship with him has been restored.

For me, the encounter I described in Reflection 10 changed everything! My immediate concern was how I was supposed to reintegrate with normal life. Should I carry on climbing distillation columns on my assignment at the oil refinery the next day, as if nothing had happened? Or should I tell everyone? This describes something of the tension I have lived with ever since, and to some extent these *Reflections* have grown out of this tension.

In many ways it *felt* like a new beginning. It also came at a time when I was considering what career to pursue. I felt I had been freed of my drive to stay with the front of the pack, which was probably driving me into business where I could continue to *do well for myself*. Instead, I now felt compelled to invite Father God into every decision, and I readied myself for an adventure. My desire to help people was now stronger than ever, and I assumed this might be leading me to work in overseas development. Ironically, as the adventure began to unfold one step at a time, I found that it was leading me into business after all, albeit according to a new design and with a new perspective.

12. Mind the Gap

"To bridge the gap between management and the shop floor."
(Chapter 5)

In theory, everyone in an organisation should know their role and should work together towards a common goal. In practice, a chief threat to this ideal is the weakness of an organisation's structure. Principal weaknesses can develop as gaps between groups of people. For example, departments are typically formed by grouping people with similar functional skills. Vertical gaps then propagate between these departments. Extra attention is needed to ensure cooperation and communication across these gaps. Alternatively, the organisation can be redesigned (e.g. along its product/service lines) so that the gaps or weaknesses do not limit cooperation or performance to the same degree.

In a typical manufacturing company, a second type of weakness is propagated across its hierarchy. This is often exacerbated by each group having different locations, wearing different uniforms and speaking different languages. Staff at head office speak "profit and cash flow", whereas people in the factory speak "people, processes and machines".

A key component of my work in manufacturing organisations is bridging and closing the gap between senior managers and the shop floor. This draws together my experiences as both a manufacturing engineer and a management consultant in order to translate the needs and constraints of each group into plain language, devoid of jargon. One of the most rewarding aspects of my work is then seeing the renewal of mutual respect and understanding. This results in a stronger organisation, where improved management goals become firmly coupled with improved shop-floor capabilities.

12. Mind the Gap

"Whoever hears my word and believes him who sent me has eternal life and will not be judged but has crossed over from death to life." (John 5v24)

Jesus used various models to explain in plain terms how his life, death and resurrection would play the critical role in restoring us to Father God. For example, he described himself as the ransom, a gate, a good shepherd, the way and the light. During my search, Christians used several of these models to try to explain the central idea to me. The problem was that I no longer seemed able to accept it, and none of these models seemed to help. I was still struggling to reconcile the credibility of Jesus with his seemingly incredible claims: that God had a son; that he had chosen to send him to earth as a man and that his death has eternal significance for someone like me two thousand years later. I could accept there was room in life for mystery, but things didn't seem to stack up. For example, if an omnipotent God existed and I needed forgiveness, why couldn't he just forgive me?

It was while I was in France that the idea dawned on me: why not ask the hypothetical Father God to explain it, if it was of importance? So this is the request I voiced, just before the encounter that changed my life. In between, my mind was filled with a vivid picture of Jesus hanging on the underside of a cross-shaped drawbridge. This had been lowered across a chasm which separated a polluted island from its unspoiled mainland. This picture instantly gripped me, to the point that I was soon counting myself among the men like ants, who were crawling home across the drawbridge. I now understand Father God to be personal, so I do not necessarily expect this particular model to grip others in the same way. I believe it is just the way that Father God chose to convict me that Jesus, permanently connected to his Father, is uniquely able to bridge the gap opened up by our sin, so that each of us can return home.

13. FAITH

"You'll only see it working when you exercise your faith in it."
(Chapter 20)

Faith is something all leaders need to exercise when making a change, simply because the future cannot be seen until it happens. Faith is required to launch a new product, to enter a new market or to adopt any new way of working. Faith is, of course, not a virtue in itself: the virtue depends on whatever you are considering putting your faith in. The sound basis for doing so can and should be tested: products can be trialled, markets can be analysed and new ways of working can be simulated. Nevertheless, faith must still be exercised by "going live".

When helping clients to design and implement new ways of working, I am sensitive to the dynamics when a client faces the prospect of going live with a new end-to-end system we have designed together. I benefit from having seen many similar solutions achieve transformation in comparable situations, but the client is in a different and potentially vulnerable position. I can show case studies, we can respond to every concern and test the solutions, but the client must ultimately find the courage to exercise their own faith for their own organisation. Sometimes this vulnerability manifests in projecting unreasonable fears on to the new solution. For example, a production manager might ask, "What if several of our machines go down?" This will, of course, present a problem to any practical system, including the typically shaky platform that the client is currently standing on – which is seldom subjected to much scrutiny. In pointing this out, clients are en*couraged* to see that rather than taking a leap into the unknown, they are actually stepping out from their shaky but familiar situation onto a new but surer foundation.

13. FAITH

"Therefore everyone who hears these words of mine and puts them into practice is like a wise man who built his house on the rock." (Matthew 7v24)

Jesus said we could be restored to Father God by exercising *faith* in him. In practice, this typically requires the hypothesis-driven approach of drawing near to Father God, counting ourselves reconciled to him through Jesus' righteousness, and welcoming God's Spirit to breathe new life into us.

In my spare time I have run several Alpha courses on behalf of local churches. These are open to everyone who wants to explore the basis for Christian faith without pressure and jargon. When run well, I like the way Alpha presents evidence for putting faith in Jesus while affording people the freedom to raise and discuss their personal concerns. While presenting information and sharing my own experiences, I am aware that after putting my faith in Jesus I have also benefitted from seeing many others encounter positive changes after doing the same. However, I recognise the vulnerability that others may face when considering their own position. This often manifests in unreasonable fears being projected on to the Christian faith. A natural response is to want to dot the i's and cross the t's before it feels *safe* to take a step of faith. However, the current belief systems of most Alpha participants have rarely been scrutinised to the same degree. Often these comprise personal collections of loose, untested ideas and hopes (e.g. "I believe in something"). Therefore people are often encouraged that putting one's faith in Jesus is less akin to taking a step out into the unknown. It is more comparable to stepping from a shaky platform of one's own ideas onto a surer foundation of Jesus' claims, which might already have been tried and tested by others you can trust.

14. Proof

"As the manager of the dye shop I can only commit to changes when I see proof that they work." (Chapter 20)

As noted in the reflection on Faith (Reflection 13), it would be foolish to attempt a significant business change without having first established evidence that supports a sound basis for it. Assurance can be taken from each test that the solution passes, especially since any of these could have exposed the solution and *disproved* its effectiveness. Nevertheless, some risk will always remain because it is normally impossible (and unnecessary) to *prove* that a new solution will work in every eventuality.

Part of my role is to help managers assemble sufficient evidence to support each change, but I have learnt to be wary if a manager continually demands more evidence or proof. Some act as if such demands are always rational, but my concerns are raised if a manager also shows no interest in the mounting evidence that *supports* the proposed change. Firstly, this can suggest a hidden desire to *disprove* the solution, perhaps because of the manager's underlying personal or political reasons to preserve the status quo. Secondly, it can suggest an unwillingness to take the plunge and commit to the changes. In many ways it can appear a safe strategy to sit on the fence and wait until a solution is completely proven. But in practice, a manager must commit to a new way of working *before* implementation, in order to *make* it work. If a manager remains unwilling to take the plunge, it is unlikely they will ever see the proof they may claim to be seeking.

14. PROOF

"A wicked and adulterous generation asks for a miraculous sign! But none will be given it except the sign of the prophet Jonah." (Matthew 12v39)

When Jesus started to make his remarkable claims, people looked for evidence that might back these up. Early such evidence or signs included Jesus demonstrating control over natural phenomena (such as healing terminal illnesses and calming storms). News of these acts spread, and many were recorded by eyewitnesses and contemporary Jewish and Roman historians. Such personal testimony is still the form of evidence that underpins much of today's judicial processes. But for some people, the witness of *other* people's stories never seems enough.

In Matthew's account some teachers approached Jesus to ask for their *own* miracle, but he refused. Perhaps Jesus saw in their request unhealthy cynicism or an expectation for him to dance to *their* tune instead of humility and openness. Instead, Jesus singled out Jonah's account of surviving for three days within a huge fish. Among all the miracles told within the people's scriptures, this may have been one of the most challenging to believe. Yet Jesus went on to claim that Jonah's miracle also foretold how *he* would spend three days in the earth, after his crucifixion. The resurrection of Jesus became his own ultimate sign: one that underpinned all his claims. The authorities knew Jesus' predictions about his resurrection and made efforts to *disprove* them by securing his grave, but were unable to produce his body. My own story now adds to the increasing evidence of those whose experiences are consistent with this resurrected life surging within them. For me, this experience now serves as sufficient personal *proof* of Jesus' claims – yet it came after I took the plunge.

15. Keep it Simple

"The solutions are brilliantly simple, but part of the brilliance has been in making them simple, so they are accessible to everyone." (Chapter 17)

Some solutions that appear simple can be completely ineffective, especially if they originate from an over-simplistic understanding of the problem. However, the simplicity of other solutions might also belie the depth of innovation and understanding that has been invested in them.

The process of understanding a business problem can involve working through successive layers of complexity. As I work with process experts to design a workable system, its components start to reflect this complexity. We need to develop theses components to address every eventuality and tie them in with existing products, equipment constraints, IT systems and other working practices. The resulting solution may be theoretically sound, but if its components have become so complex that it can't be implemented or followed, it will be no good at all. Therefore we need to invest still further resources to develop each complex component into one that can be simple to communicate and follow. For example, if a production process has complex scheduling and sequencing constraints, more work is needed to design a failsafe way to channel waiting products into the prescribed, optimal sequence. This can often be achieved by designing a custom, simple and visual scheduling board and intuitive rules that bypass the complexity. It is normally much harder to develop a workable solution in such a way so that it *appears* simple than a solution that looks complicated. However, the greatest of workable solutions *requires* this simplicity, despite the layers of complexity that will be hidden within it.

15. KEEP IT SIMPLE

"You have hidden these things from the wise and learned, and revealed them to little children." (Matthew 11v25)

Jesus repeatedly emphasised that we could know God and enter fullness of life, simply by putting our faith in him and in what he would accomplish. Could it really be that simple?

The picture of a drawbridge (Reflection 12) helped me to personally make enough sense of Jesus' claims, and moved me to put my faith in them. What I then encountered compelled me to start telling friends and family. But although I could describe how everything had come alive for me, I did not seem very effective in bringing fresh insight to others. I felt no more able to explain Jesus' claims with conclusive wisdom. To be honest, I still found myself thinking that my case sounded a bit simplistic.

Through further years of trying to make sense of everything, I discovered several layers to the solution of the death and resurrection of Jesus. For example, it reveals the nature and extent of God's characteristics, which we all reflect to some degree as created beings. He is entirely just (in refusing to ignore consequences), entirely loving (in sacrificing what was most precious), entirely powerful (in suspending natural laws) and eternal (in revealing life beyond death). Yet each of us is also unique. I would argue it is extremely unlikely that an omnipotent Father God would have chosen to design life in such a way that he could only be known by the "wise and learned". I think it much more likely that a loving Father God has chosen to be accessed equally by all, through the simplest of solutions. Sadly, this may therefore mean that the wise and learned might struggle the most, *because* the solution requires faith alone. It requires nothing of the wisdom and learning in which many of us take so much pride.

16. ROLL-OUT?

"The better you become at respecting and influencing individuals, the better you will be at effecting sustainable change – and igniting a positive culture."
(Chapter 18)

When a pilot transformation proves successful, a tremendous sense of celebration is typically shared between leaders, change agents, local managers and the rest of the workforce who have all worked together. It is a great feeling: the enthusiasm seems infectious, and leaders and change agents are eager to spread the transformation to the rest of the business.

While celebrating the success of a pilot transformation, I often need to remind people of the journey they have come through. Otherwise their enthusiasm can be channelled into a desire to roll out the transformation immediately to the rest of the business. It is important to remind people that the pilot's success has been forged through the combination of relevant insight, practical change-management and good leadership. If the relevant insight is overlooked in subsequent transformation attempts, change agents may try to copy and paste solutions into further areas instead of understanding and solving its own problems. If change-management is overlooked, it might be forgotten that each new area is run by different managers and employees who need to be respected and engaged as individuals, just as they were in the pilot area. If the need for good leadership is overlooked, leaders may withdraw after the spotlight of the pilot, and become less available or less inclined to remove the specific obstacles limiting improvement in the rest of the business. Enthusiasm can be infectious, but without sensitivity it can also grate. Ultimately, transformation is facilitated by respecting people as individuals, helping them to solve their pressing problems, removing obstacles and bringing insight to help them thrive.

16. ROLL-OUT?

"Flesh gives birth to flesh, but the Spirit gives birth to spirit ... The wind blows wherever it pleases ... So it is with everyone born of the Spirit."
(John 3v6,8)

Jesus said that the agent of spiritual transformation is the Spirit of his Father God: the Holy Spirit. This is the same Spirit who he said dwelled within him, and who he said would bring life to and dwell within every individual who believes in him. He compared this Spirit to the wind, which blows wherever it pleases.

My encounter had provided me with personal evidence that God was alive: his Spirit was alive within me. My instant response was to ask, why hadn't anyone *told me* that this was possible?

The truth, of course, is that many people *had* told me, albeit in a crowded, noisy world. If people had told me with enthusiasm, I had probably been suspicious of them. Yet if they had lacked enthusiasm, I would probably have dismissed them for not practising what they preached! With hindsight, I realise that spiritual transformation was not something that anyone could have *rolled out* to me. Although people can play an important part, the principal change agent for spiritual transformation is Father God's Spirit. Like the wind, he cannot be bound by formulae. Saul of Tarsus provides dramatic, early evidence of this. He was transformed in a single, *uninvited* encounter: from infamous persecutor of early Christians to Paul, the famous Christian leader who was willing to *embrace* persecution to communicate his new faith in Jesus. However, also like the wind, God's Spirit can be anticipated. Therefore we can set our sails by inviting him to lead us on our own, personal change journey.

17. Higher Power

"In you we have a leader who can make things happen."
(Chapter 27)

When I worked as a project manager within CarnaudMetalbox (which was later acquired by Crown Cork), I was used to working within corporate guidelines, like its travel policy, that seemed to be set in stone. I understood that the policy was necessary to ensure good use of resources, but working within its constraints sometimes proved frustrating. For example, I once had to negotiate for a supplier to cover the cost of my short flight so that I could investigate some equipment first-hand.

After completing my training in McKinsey's Production System Design Centre, I began to work for more typical McKinsey clients which were similar in size to CarnaudMetalbox. The main difference was that I was now working on projects that were of the highest priority to those at the top of the organisation. Having been conditioned by working at the bottom and in the middle of corporations, I was shocked when I was able to take the next transatlantic flight to visit a client's supplier as soon as the need arose. Travel policies still existed, but I was now working for people with the authority, power and desire to make things happen quickly, even if it occasionally meant lifting the rules that they themselves had put in place.

17. Higher Power

"You are in error because you do not know the Scriptures or the power of God." (Matthew 22v29)

Jesus drew large crowds because of what he did as well as what he said. For example, as noted in Reflection 14, he healed the sick and exercised power over the weather. Such events are described as miracles because they cannot be explained by natural laws. Because most of what we witness day to day has been shaped by these natural laws, it can seem that they are set in stone. Yet it also seems reasonable that if an omnipotent creator God exists, he might grant himself the possibility and power to suspend or work beyond the natural laws that he himself put in place.

In Reflection 6 I mentioned that during my quest I had asked Father God to arrange some voluntary work for me overseas. I hadn't really expected that he could or would, so I dismissed it as a coincidence when a friend started telling me about Jackie Pullinger, a British Christian who still works with drug addicts in Hong Kong. After giving up on the idea of voluntary work I booked my ticket to Hong Kong where I planned to meet friends before travelling around China. Then in France, after the encounter that changed my life, I sought out a church in which to worship my Father God. During the service I felt compelled to speak to the two people in front of me. They invited me to have lunch with them, and it transpired that I had been getting to know Jackie Pullinger's sister and nephew. My Father God had somehow orchestrated people, timing and events to make things happen. I shared most of the rest of my wonderful summer with remarkable men in Hong Kong who were discovering new life after years of addiction to hard drugs. Beyond my initial encounter, this was my first tangible sense of a Higher Power operating in my life, working things out in unfathomable ways to prepare a better life than I could have planned for myself.

18. Exercising Authority

"Josh appealed to Peter and Trevor for either of them to apply their authority as line managers." (Chapter 19)

Every decision to change something within an organisation must be made through the organisation's chain of command: never by a consultant or a change agent. For example, the decision to change the way people work within a specific area must be taken by that area's manager. In this way, managers can continue to manage their areas, factor the changes into other aspects of doing so, and take responsibility for sustaining the integrated new ways of working.

The term "chain of command" is not perfect, since leaders of civilian organisations should not expect to pass "commands" through their hierarchy in the same way that leaders of military organisations might. Nevertheless, the term can be useful to convey the hierarchy of successive line managers that exists in most organisations, through which authority is delegated. An important principle is that none of these line managers has any authority other than that which has been delegated from the top. To facilitate transformation, I need to work with every individual in this chain, to ensure they approve of the decisions and *how* they are being made.

A central challenge is that a transformation initiative stresses and tests a chain of command like never before. It tends to expose managers who have perhaps been unwilling to exercise the authority that has been delegated to them. Therefore a major part of facilitating transformation is coaching and strengthening managers to analyse, engage and implement changes that make sense, while delegating the authority and entrusting others to make the types of decisions that they are best qualified to make.

18. EXERCISING AUTHORITY

"Go! Let it be done just as you believed it would."
(Matthew 8v13)

A Roman centurion said to Jesus, "Just say the word, and my servant will be healed. For I myself am a man under authority, with soldiers under me." He appears to refer to the *authority* that Jesus exercised to heal, which his Father had delegated to him. Jesus commended the centurion for his faith, and his servant was indeed healed. Later, Jesus told his followers, "Whoever believes in me will do the works I have been doing" (John 14v12). He was implying that Father God's authority would be delegated to all believers. Ever since, there have been accounts of Jesus' followers exercising the authority to heal in this way.

I have always found it relatively easy to join in with general prayers for healing. It feels more awkward to personally offer to pray for someone's healing, particularly if nothing appeared to happen the last time. *Exercising* the authority Jesus delegates to us involves risks, embracing vulnerability and, frankly, it often seems easier to avoid it and do nothing. Yet I feel that being avoidant will not help me to live life to the full and practise what I believe, in the face of need. I can't explain why I don't always see healing, but I am very thankful whenever I do. Sometimes when I pray for people my hands grow hot as a sign that something is happening. For example, this happened while praying for the knee of a friend I had met through playing football. Doctors had told him that he would never be able to run or cycle again, and I sensed that a mutual friend and I needed to pray for him. The lump on his knee disappeared: he is enjoying sport again and recently completed a 10k race with no pain! I have much to learn through further practice in this area, and I greatly respect those I know who are much further ahead in exercising the authority that God delegates to us.

19. Change Journey

"Work deeply with everyone through phases to diagnose, design, implement and refine new ways of working." (Chapter 9)

The process I practise for managing change is similar to the one first demonstrated to me. It consists of four phases: diagnose, design, implement and refine. The first reason I love this model is because of its simplicity: it provides a straightforward means to communicate and explain the process of change to everyone in an organisation. Because it is simple, it can be recalled easily, which helps everyone to register where they are within an overall, transparent process. Secondly, the progression of these activities prescribes a healthy, logical route to engage and lead people through change. For example, it is important to diagnose the overall problem before continuing to work together to design an overall solution.

Diagnose: to clarify the need, to set rough objectives and to analyse data to confirm whether there is enough opportunity to meet the need.

Design: to develop from scratch a holistic new way of working; to adapt it around constraints; to test it with data to confirm whether the objectives can be met and to plan how each part of the solution should be implemented.

Implement: to make the physical changes and to coach people with the new ways of working.

Refine: to help people to prioritise and solve problems that the new system causes or exposes, and to continue to improve the solution to simplify it and/or capture more of the available opportunity.

19. Change Journey

"For God so loved the world that he gave his one and only Son, that whoever believes in him shall not perish but have eternal life." (John 3v16)

Jesus said that whoever believes in him would go through a change of eternal significance. Through these right-hand reflections I have outlined elements of my own journey, after setting out to make sense of Jesus' claims for myself. I haven't always been able to see the big picture (including my original need for change), but the four-stage process helps me to reflect on the main aspects of my transformation to date:

Diagnose: in one sense, "perishing" describes the fate of death that awaits all of us. It also describes the condition I now see I was in without the breath of God's Spirit in me. Although I was unaware of this, I did sense there could be more in the claims of Jesus than I had yet encountered.

Design: I believe the design is rooted in Father God's love for each of us. Firstly, his design solves the problem, through Jesus, of our separation from him caused by our sin. Secondly, his plan is for each of us to partner with him to live out our uniquely designed life to the full.

Implement: God's Spirit is the change agent who can be invited to make everything a personal reality. The typical process involves taking ownership of our own problem, asking for forgiveness and exercising faith in Jesus.

Refine: in reality, I find that the implement and refine phases are continuously interleaved, as God continues to refine my character and release me to greater fullness of life. The adventure goes on as I learn to welcome and partner with God's Spirit within me to surface and solve further problems in me and in the world around me.

20. Unconscious Incompetence

"You didn't know how much there was to know about designing an operation." (Chapter 14)

Before a McKinsey expert demonstrated to me the art of transformation, I thought I was relatively well prepared, having worked on improvements in dozens of facilities. With hindsight, I can now see that my pride was blocking further learning: I had no idea how much more there was to know. Now, after sixteen years of transforming operations and cultures, I still regularly gain a fresh awareness of how much more there is to learn.

You might be able to reflect on similar learning cycles in your own areas of expertise. I find this cycle is represented well through the model that was first publicised by Gordon Training International:

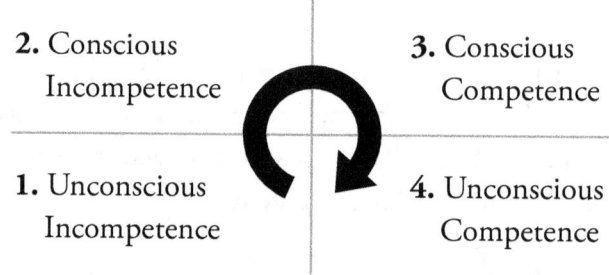

1. We often start with no idea how much we have yet to know.
2. It can then be daunting as we discover how much we don't yet know.
3. As we learn by doing, we become aware of our growing skills.
4. As we continue to practise, the skills become second nature… and we start the next cycle.

This model structures my expectations as I prepare to enter any new field or industry, and helps to normalise the experiences of those I train.

20. Unconscious Incompetence

"Are you not in error because you do not know the Scriptures or the power of God?" (Mark 12v24)

Jesus attracted different types of people who seemed unprepared to learn. Some seemed intent on showing *him* how much they knew, while others were intent on trapping him. Many of these did already know quite a bit about the Jewish scriptures, so Jesus risked their wrath by challenging how much they really knew. On another occasion he said to a group that diligently studied the scriptures, "These are the very Scriptures that testify about me, yet you refuse to come to me to have life" (John 5v39,40). It was as if their initial learning had blocked further discovery: they had no idea how much there was still to know.

I think I can relate to these people to some degree. I remember thinking I already knew quite a bit about Jesus. I would have recognised that there was more I could have learned *about* Jesus, but I had no idea how much *more* was available. The encounter that I described in Reflection 10 suddenly propelled me to a whole new plane that I had no idea existed. This discovery was so profound that I remember thinking immediately afterwards, "This is it! I have discovered life's great secret!" In that moment there seemed little else to discover.

Twenty-three years later, I am still discovering more about myself, what it means to live life to the full, and about Father God, Jesus and God's Spirit. I sometimes feel that I have come so far that it is difficult to relate to my old self. Yet when I find myself on the brink of another cycle of discovery, it can feel like I have barely begun.

21. Narrow and Deep

"A narrow and deep approach is the proven path to sustainable transformation." (Chapter 9)

The transformation approach which I continue to advocate can be described as "narrow and deep". Most commonly, I apply this to help workforces to transform their results and culture by redesigning how people work throughout an end-to-end operation. This requires *deep* work in designing new procedures that are applicable to all products and processes, and *deep* coaching to convince, involve and support people through implementation. This depth of work requires a significant full-time team of change agents, so it is normally prudent to limit the size of this team and focus it on a limited scope. It is important that this scope constitutes a *narrow* slice through the organisation: one defined around an end-to-end flow through the operation, so that systems can be designed to collapse the inevitable wastes that will have been caused by constraints to flow. Once change agents have learnt to facilitate transformation in the first slice, they can move on to transform the next narrow and deep slice.

It can be challenging to convince people of the need for such an approach to transformation, particularly if they have limited experience of what it takes to transform how a workforce thinks and behaves. Clients sometimes want to leverage their investment by trying to change the whole organisation at once. Broad and deep sounds wonderful. But effecting *deep* change across the whole operation would require a multiplication of resources, and other constraints (such as the availability of leadership) might then threaten its success. Other improvement approaches (which typically impart skills instead of prescribing and implementing detailed changes) *are* suited to broader scopes. These can still deliver good value – but in my experience are unlikely to ever achieve transformation.

21. Narrow and Deep

"But small is the gate and narrow the road that leads to life, and only a few find it." (Matthew 7v14)

The number one priority for life that Jesus commends to us is to love Father God with all of our heart, soul, mind and strength (Mark 12v30). This requires *deep* transformation, particularly because many people begin their spiritual journeys unconvinced as to whether God even exists. Yet even to those Jesus addressed who would typically have believed in God, he declared that the road leading to life was narrow and few would find it.

Why did Jesus say the path to deep transformation was also "narrow"? He contrasts this with a wide gate and broad road that leads to destruction (Matthew 7v13), implying that those following the more obvious route will forgo salvation. Jesus' path is not narrow in terms of exclusivity: it is available to everyone, but it does pass through a narrow gate. Elsewhere Jesus claimed that he *is* the gate, saying, "Whoever enters through me will be saved" (John 10v9).

The role of the gate is related to Jesus' claims about his crucifixion and resurrection (See Reflection 12): only through him could the problem of separation from Father God be solved. I have often contemplated why the path leading to the Creator of the Universe should be so narrow. Shouldn't the route somehow appear more *successful*: perhaps wider, more obvious and better travelled? I am beginning to see that the answer might be exposed in this very type of thinking, which still tends to value breadth above depth. Perhaps I have still not begun to grasp the depth of Father God's love which would sacrifice everything to afford any one of us the freedom to choose to love *him*.

22. Tied-up Capital

"Don't consider inventory as something to keep topped up!"
(Chapter 8)

Most business investors share the basic goal of achieving a good return on their capital. In a manufacturing business, much of this capital is tied up in inventory: raw material, work-in-process and finished goods along the supply chain. Therefore if an operation could be redesigned to safely collapse the inventory required, you might think that managers would seize this opportunity to bolster the overall return on capital employed and/or to liberate cash for further opportunities.

I continue to learn that the dynamics of a manufacturing business are much more complicated beneath the surface! In reality, people at every level commonly have attachments to inventory, for different reasons. Senior managers are often more incentivised to improve the absolute return. Furthermore, according to accounting protocol, the reported return will actually take a *hit* in any period in which inventory is reduced. Middle managers are often focused to meet productivity targets which tend to be easier to achieve with higher inventory (e.g. with larger batches). There is also a general sense in which people like inventory because it makes a facility *feel* busy. The owner of one client once admitted to me that he *liked* to see his factory full of inventory because when he showed customers around it made it look like they were "doing well"!

It often proves difficult to transform a business unless unhealthy attachments to inventory can be exposed and tackled as part of the transformation process. Then, by weaning itself off these attachments, the business will begin to enjoy more of its potential and prove how much of this potential had in fact been *tied up* – by how its capital was being used.

22. Tied-up Capital

"Life does not consist in an abundance of possessions."
(Luke 12v15)

The desire to acquire possessions and to build personal wealth is not new. Two thousand years ago Jesus frequently warned people against greed, because fullness of life is not to be found in wealth.

Today the desire to build personal wealth appears as strong as ever, as suggested by the demand for business books offering advice on "how to get rich". Most people I know would not claim to seek wealth for its own sake, and would probably agree that wealth in itself does not bring fullness of life. Yet personal wealth is still seen as a sign of success and an indication that someone is "doing well". If we are not careful, this becomes a hook, where our desire to "do well" (or to be seen to be doing well) influences our decisions. This warning was unwittingly etched in me by corporate recruiters at university, who hailed a recruit from a few years earlier as a role model who was "doing exceptionally well". True, he had already secured a senior role but he did not look happy: it transpired that his choices had already contributed to the break-up of his young marriage.

Although wealth appears to offer greater freedom and control over our circumstances, our love of wealth can end up controlling *us*. It can control our choices, cost us what we value most and hinder our pursuit of the fullness of life that deep down, we may desire the most. This is why Jesus warned that the love of money can become like a god, and while in its grasp we are not free to pursue Father God or the fullness of life he offers. Jesus said he can help to set us "free indeed" from such attachments (John 8v36). "You cannot serve both God and money," he said, "For where your treasure is, there your heart will be also" (Matthew 6v24,21).

23. Surfacing and Solving

"We need to solve problems instead of burying them with waste, like excess inventory, equipment or lead times." (Chapter 8)

I have witnessed how some organisations like to present themselves as problem-free. Yet all organisations have problems, if a problem is broadly identified by any gap between desired and existing situations. A machine may break down, a delivery may be missed or someone may feel that their full contribution has not been welcomed. To me, the mark of an organisation's strength is what it chooses to do with such problems.

When a problem occurs, there is normally pressure just to keep going. As a result, many organisations bury their problems without understanding and solving the root causes. Most problems can be covered up by throwing money at them (e.g. replacing machine parts instead of understanding why they keep failing). Or resources can be thrown at mitigating the effect of the problem somewhere else (e.g. building excess inventory to protect downstream processes from an unreliable machine). Either way, buried problems result in a double whammy. Firstly, the potential of the business is hampered because the buried problem remains unsolved. Secondly, performance deteriorates further because of the resources wasted in covering it up.

In the light of this, every leader has a choice. Does he or she want to preside over an organisation that *looks* polished and problem-free to outsiders? Or is it willing to look a little messier, while deliberately surfacing and solving its problems? It is by risking the latter approach that an organisation can develop its internal strength and begin to fulfil its true potential.

23. SURFACING AND SOLVING

"Come to me, all you who are weary and burdened, and I will give you rest."
(Matthew 11v28)

The fullness of life that Jesus offers involves more than forgiving our past and saving our future: he can help us very practically to improve our lives in the here and now. He *exhorts* those of us who have become wearied with life to come to him, so that he can unburden us.

Jesus is invested in surfacing and healing our buried problems. These are caused by things in life that we would never have wanted to encounter, ranging from disappointments to broken relationships to serious abuse. These are normally very difficult to deal with at the time: the most expedient approach is often to bury them in an effort to get on with life as best we can. Sadly, the buried problems can end up shaping our whole life and potential – often subconsciously. Firstly, they can pollute our core beliefs about ourselves. Secondly, they can waste inordinate private thoughts and energy, such as in covering them up to appear well, or with habits we develop as compensating mechanisms. Thirdly, they can produce an unhealthy drive, founded on insecurity.

Jesus recognised the root causes of specific burdens being carried by people who approached him. He also demonstrated the compassion, power and resources to set them free. Further testimonies have continued ever since, from people who have been set free from all types of burdens. In fact, one of my greatest privileges as a Christian has been getting to know so many people who come to life as they recount how Father God has healed and unburdened them from afflictions and buried memories that have shaped and limited their lives for years.

24. Continuous Improvement

"The transformation won't be finished until we run out of problems to surface and solve." (Chapter 30)

Towards the end of a transformation initiative's implementation phase, the workplace should be looking and performing much better. It can be exhilarating for people to see the designed changes working and the exposed problems being solved. I need to prepare them for this sense of accomplishment, to prevent them from falling into the trap of thinking the transformation has been completed. In fact, they should consider it as having just begun. The point here is not to engage in mind games to keep everyone striving for more, but to transform mindsets so the *fruit* of transformation can be enjoyed, which is continuous improvement.

The designed changes will typically feature visual management. This enables everyone to tell at a glance where and when support is required. These systems then need to be put to continuous good use, so that further, priority problems are surfaced and solved at the right pace, one after another. It is likely that most of these surfaced problems (e.g. excess inventory or an oil leak) might never have been noticed or considered a problem before. Therefore a prerequisite for dealing with them must be a supportive culture. This should have been modelled through the change journey and by coaching leaders where necessary to do the same. Then, far from the workforce feeling burdened with "extra" or "unnecessary" problems, the continuous improvement cycle becomes a virtuous cycle. People can thrive, through continually contributing and developing more of their skills, while continually strengthening the organisation's capability and performance.

24. Continuous Improvement

"Sanctify them by the truth; your word is truth."
(John 17v17)

When Jesus was facing arrest, he prayed for those who had put their faith in him. He asked Father God to "sanctify" them by the truth. This term conveys the process of setting apart, making holy and purifying. Jesus understood that God's word – which he called truth – would be his means for facilitating this.

As I described in Reflection 7, after measuring myself against standards in the Bible ("God's word"), I considered I was OK: I did not think I had any significant problems to address. It was *after* my transforming encounter that I saw God's standards in a new light. For example, when I measured the best love I could generate against my experience of *God's* love, mine no longer seemed very generous! So began a process that has continued ever since. Each cycle begins with my honest confession about a way in which I have fallen short of God's standard for mankind – as outlined in the Bible – and I begin to ask for his help to solve the lack or problem in me that this reveals. Occasionally the revelation and improvement feels so significant that it seems I have reached a plateau. The process is then quickly restored by asking God to reveal more sin in me that needs to be dealt with. Often this is revealed through motivations, or thoughts I have dwelt on. God's love ensures that it does not feel condemnatory: I know that I have been forgiven, based on Jesus having met the standard on my behalf. Instead, the focus is for me to fulfil more of my potential. It is deeply fulfilling to sense Father God's continuous improvement process at work, helping me to become the person he created me to be, and less swayed by others. I am now twenty-three years into this process of sanctification, but it still sometimes feels that I have barely begun.

25. THE FREEDOM PARADOX

"The process has trapped itself in this mess because of the lack of instruction ... These are the steps that can set it free!" (Chapter 16)

When I start working with a typical production supervisor, they tend to value their *freedom* to run their facility "flexibly". This tends to mean however they see fit, based on their experience. Existing schedules are supposed to dictate when each product should go through which process, but often these do not take into account the capabilities and constraints of individual processes. Therefore the supervisor is authorised to override the schedule. However, by prioritising one product, they unintentionally deprioritise another, which they may then have to expedite, and so on. Therefore the freedom which a supervisor sets out to enjoy often ends up *trapping* them – and the entire facility – in chaotic activity. A non-flexible, damaging mode of firefighting prevails.

A core component of improving an end-to-end operation is designing a better scheduling method. Typically, this involves applying local experience to design rules for each process to prescribe which of the waiting products should be scheduled next. These designs factor in the specific constraints and capacities of each process, while guaranteeing a maximum wait time. This brings predictability to the overall operation, which helps to guarantee delivery performance. Furthermore, by reducing the maximum process wait times, the overall lead time through the facility (and the associated inventory) can typically be halved. Further still, since the operators can follow the rules by themselves, the supervisor's time can be freed to focus on things that matter, including continuous improvement. The first step towards all these benefits, though, is to build enough trust with the supervisor to overcome the apparent paradox: that he – and the facility as a whole – can be set free with the help of some carefully designed rules.

25. THE FREEDOM PARADOX

"Very truly I tell you, everyone who sins is a slave to sin."
(John 8v34)

Jesus insisted that everyone who sins is a slave to sin. Afterwards, he said, "If the Son sets you free, you will be free indeed" (John 8v36). When I was younger there seemed a clear paradox here. I associated Jesus' teaching about sin and commandments with discipline, which seemed the antithesis of freedom. Jesus took the commandments a step further by teaching that sin occurred not just through acts but also in the heart and mind. For example, he taught that dwelling on lustful or hateful thoughts had the same root as committing adultery or murder. I could accept the need for some discipline, but surely this was excessively restrictive? It seemed more appealing to think that everyone should just lighten up and have fun, so long as they didn't hurt anyone.

My perspective began to change the moment I encountered Father God's love: if everyone's heart could be filled with the love I was experiencing, it was evident that all the world's problems would be solved. I had tasted what an entirely good God might be like. What, then, if everything we value and take pleasure from in life has been created by him, out of this love? The paradox is then solved when we begin to see Jesus' guidelines as helping us to make the most of these good gifts. For example, dwelling on hateful or lustful thoughts can prevent us from loving well and can rob our hearts of joy. I imagine all of us have also been trapped by the harmful *effects* of our own sin in some way: in addictive patterns of thinking or behaviour; by private shame; with painful consequences of our actions or by wrong beliefs about ourselves. Jesus said he could set us free indeed: not just from eternal consequences of sin, but by helping us to follow God's guidelines for enjoying more of his good gifts for life, right now.

26. CONTROL ISSUE

"Too tight a grip can suffocate."
(Chapter 13)

I have worked with a broad spectrum of factory managers, ranging from one who readily offered that he was not at all in control to those who exuded very keenly their need to *maintain* control. The latter manager often makes a good first impression, but as well as presenting potential difficulties for the change journey, there are several ways in which a manager's excessive grip might have already limited business performance.

First, a manager who places too great an emphasis on control may unwittingly pressurise others to report only what they think the manager wants to hear. Problems can be suppressed, along with opportunities to improve. Second, rigid focus on a manager's own agenda can suppress good ideas and potential from elsewhere. Third, a manager's controlling nature can condition others to play to the rules instead of doing the right thing. For example, if a direct report has not "used up" his entire budget this year, they may find lesser needs to spend it on before the money is "lost". Fourth, by stating that "targets must be met at all costs", a manager may be inviting exactly that. For example, under-pressure managers can put their own staff under intense pressure to meet short-term targets. I have known this to result in factory personnel expediting all high-value orders and even cancelling deliveries of raw materials. Even if they "make the month", morale and long-term performance can be damaged, while ironically driving the factory *out* of control.

Where a manager takes pride in their control of the business, careful coaching is required: unless they learn to loosen their grip in the right ways, they may never breathe life into the improvements they seek.

26. Control Issue

"For whoever wants to save their life will lose it, but whoever loses their life for me will find it." (Matthew 16v25)

When Jesus said that he was going to be executed, his friend Peter took him aside and said, "This shall never happen to you!" (Matthew 16v22). Jesus rebuked him, saying "You do not have in mind the concerns of God, but merely human concerns." The implication was that in trying to take control of that situation, Peter was opposing God's will. Jesus then generalised this point by implying that those determined to maintain control of their own life will lose it. But those who loosen their grip to allow Jesus to steer will find it.

I used to find it empowering to think that no one could stop me living the life I wanted to live. It felt good to be in control. I could work towards doing whatever I wanted, wherever I wanted, and with whomever I wanted. The problem was that deep down, I didn't really *know* what I wanted! I could see that visions I was considering were shaped by other influences, such as a drive to prove my capabilities rather than my personal vision for a balanced, fulfilled life. Yet without any vision, I risked being steered by opportunities that came my way.

Yielding control can seem preposterous – unless somehow we can yield to one who is entirely good, knowing and powerful: who has our best interests at heart. On discovering this person in Father God, inviting him into my decisions required vulnerability, but it also made sense. With the security of his *approval* I no longer felt such a drive to *prove* my capabilities for my own sake. I look back on a good adventure so far and forward to a hopeful future. Just as life is released into any healthy relationship when we dare to exercise trust, so it is with Father God.

A J Sheppard

27. No Uncertain Terms

"Haven't we already done lean manufacturing?"
(Chapter 29)

As mentioned in Reflection 7, the Toyota Production System continues to be respected around the world for its influence on operations management. Although its innovative thinking dates back to the 1940s, in the late 1980s a new term – "lean manufacturing" – was coined to describe it. This term was then popularised by Womack and Jones through their book, *The Machine that Changed the World* (1990).

The "lean" I discovered at university and practised as an engineer shared similarities, but fell short of the lean that I went on to learn from an expert who had worked for Toyota. He preferred to avoid the term "lean", which within a few years already meant different things to different people. How could this have happened? Firstly, I think there is a risk that when anything becomes popular, its terms will be embraced as jargon faster than they can be understood. Secondly, there is a particular risk that a term based on *unseen* principles will inevitably become associated with its visible out-workings. Therefore many have learnt to see lean as a menu of solutions, and overlook the unseen importance of designing systems or changing cultures. Benefits may then be marginal at best: copying and pasting the wrong lean solution can even *increase* waste and/or damage culture. For example, a supermarket of neatly organised inventory on a shop floor can be a vital component of some lean designs, but in many make-to-order facilities it can unnecessarily waste inventory and associated costs.

One consequence of this misunderstanding is that any claim that lean has been implemented cannot be taken at face value. A better indication is in the fruit: whether a facility's performance and people appear to be thriving.

27. No Uncertain Terms

"These people honour me with their lips, but their hearts are far from me."
(Matthew 15v8)

Religious teachers often criticised Jesus for not following their religious customs and practices. Jesus incurred their wrath by calling them hypocrites: that their hearts were far from God. He went on to emphasise that it was not through adopting certain practices that someone could become clean or righteous: their heart needed to be made right first.

After the death and resurrection of Jesus, the term "Christian" was coined to describe those who put their faith in him as the *Christ* (which means "anointed one of God".) The Christianity I practised in my youth shared similarities but appeared to fall short of the Christianity I went on to encounter. Christianity, of course, means many different things to different people. I can now understand how this has happened in the light of *unseen* faith being at its core. Christianity has inevitably become associated with its out-workings that can be *seen*. These include the practices, the organisations and the buildings rather than the internal transformations that give any of these life. For these reasons I now often prefer to talk about my faith in Jesus instead of my Christianity. However, I have also met people whose ideas about *Jesus* completely misrepresent him. For example, some view Jesus as a figurehead for the type of hypocritical religious practice that aggravates them. The reality is that Jesus *hated* religious hypocrisy – so much that he was prepared to be executed for speaking out against it!

Rather than viewing customs and practices with suspicion or taking uncertain terms at face value, Jesus commended us to look beyond these, for good "fruit" in people's lives as evidence of Father God working in their hearts (Matthew 7v20).

28. Under Construction

"The new way of operating won't cause this problem. But yes, it might expose it, so that we can begin to address it." (Chapter 8)

A transformation often requires and is partially delivered through surfacing and solving problems that have been buried for a long time (Reflection 23). Continuous improvement can then be achieved by successively surfacing and solving gaps to improved standards (Reflection 24). Surfacing and solving both types of problems can prove messy work, and part of my role is to prepare managers for a state that may initially seem unpalatable to some, where problems and change are always evident.

Firstly, the organisation's capability in surfacing, prioritising and solving problems needs to be developed. For low-level problems this means developing healthy management structures and reviews, a positive culture and problem-solving skills. For deeper-set problems, a cross-functional change-management initiative might also be needed. Secondly, if an organisation used to pride itself on being sorted, it will be necessary to prepare the workforce for a cultural shock. For example, a manager might have previously been able to walk through a facility and have seen no particular needs: now on a similar walk many problems will be evident. Without proper preparation, this shift can feel uncomfortable and be quickly misunderstood – why should anyone persist with an initiative that brings no end of problems? Workforces often need help to differentiate between problems that have been *caused* by the new systems and those that would previously have existed which the new systems are now carefully and deliberately *exposing*, so that they can be solved. They should also see that this is a necessary step towards fulfilling more of their potential and moving beyond a more stagnant state that may have nevertheless *looked* problem-free.

28. Under Construction

"I have given them the glory that you gave me, that they may be one as we are one." (John 17v22)

Through his death and resurrection, Jesus said he had completed the once-for-all work of paving the way for mankind to be restored to Father God. Jesus then commissioned those who had been restored to God through him to continue this process of revelation and reconciliation. The change agent for this process – God's Spirit – had already been entrusted to them. Collectively these Christian followers became known as "the church".

Wherever I have lived or travelled, I have found local expressions of the church that I have generally enjoyed being part of, and I love the varied personal and social transformations they help to enable. Since encountering the love of Father God more personally, I have felt more compelled to regard the church as family and I have grown to love diverse expressions of worship, which play a large part in giving churches different flavours. I recognise this as the unifying work of God's Spirit within me, just as Jesus commissioned. However, disagreement and division also exist within the church. I know some people who have been put off by this, and by one or two churchgoers they would rather avoid. But I find it necessary to point out that such problems are not *caused* by Jesus. In fact, because churches are open to everyone they can serve as good training grounds where we can practise loving all types of people, just as Jesus commended. It can also be helpful to point out that in acknowledging their need for Jesus, every Christian has made an admission that they have *not* got everything sorted: they are under reconstruction. My life has been greatly enriched by getting to know many such people through varied churches. Many have become trusted friends: we are mutually invested in helping each other to fulfil more of our potential – as works in process.

29. OUT OF SIGHT

"Everything he and Linda possessed ... had come from money handed over for their products instead of competitors' products in moments like this."
(Chapter 6)

When I worked for Crown Cork I gained an appreciation of how much work was involved in producing and developing the humble tin can. I have great respect for the human ingenuity that has designed and built equipment capable of perfectly forming, welding and sealing five hundred cans every minute, for just a few pence each. I was involved in a tiny fraction of the effort that was being invested in developing this equipment so that it could produce stronger cans out of thinner plate. It therefore seemed a travesty that the typical consumer discarded each can immediately after use, without a thought for all the effort that had gone into creating it. Yet the reality is that because all this effort is out of a consumer's sight, it is also readily out of mind.

There is a related risk for people working *within* manufacturing facilities. Here, it is the customer who is out of sight and therefore readily out of mind. A false sense of security can then set in, while the workforce keeps turning out products with little appreciation of the customer. This belies the typical reality that every employee buys the very food on which they survive with money that has first been handed over by customers for their products in the marketplace, in preference to competitors' products. Without these customers, everything would stop. Such a heightened awareness of this out-of-sight dependency can expose the fragility of a business. Yet it can also lead to an increased appreciation of the customers on whom they depend, which can help the organisation to thrive.

29. OUT OF SIGHT

"Because you have seen me, you have believed; blessed are those who have not seen and yet have believed." (John 20v29)

After Jesus was executed, his closest followers were sheltered together in hiding, in fear for their own lives. The resurrected Jesus then visited them, but Thomas, who was not with them, refused to believe. A week later, Jesus visited them again when Thomas was present. Thomas reached out and touched Jesus, and he believed. This prompted Jesus to bless those who managed to put their faith in him without seeing him. He went on to explain that he would soon be rejoining his Father God out of sight, remaining present in the world through his Spirit.

There is probably something of Thomas in us all: we would rather *see* something to believe in it. There remains much evidence we *can* see and consider, but much of this can readily slip outside our day-to-day mindfulness. For example, every day our existence depends on air, food and water. While reading this page you will already have depended on several breaths. Heightened awareness of such dependency can expose our fragility. Yet it can also lead to an increased appreciation of life itself, and of whoever may be behind it, albeit out of sight. Science can help us to appreciate many intricacies of the natural world, although it will always fall short of *proving* whether there is a supernatural God to thank for everything we depend on, every second of every day.

Similarly, it is relatively easy to let the evidence of the eyewitness accounts of Jesus' life slip out of sight and mind, together with those whose lives continue to be transformed by putting their faith in Jesus. However, I would suggest we would do better to keep it where we can grapple with it, especially if life in all fullness may depend on it.

30. Fear of Change

"Even if his ideas worked over there, it doesn't mean they're going to work over here." (Chapter 20)

Many of the leaders I work with become energised by the vision we develop for their organisation. This can feed impatience, and sometimes a predisposition to group together anyone offering resistance to new ideas as being *afraid of change*. My challenge is to help leaders to slow down and engage with the resistance. Some people may indeed be fearful of change, but even then it is important to understand *why* they may be fearful. Many people take the risk of speaking out only because they care. These are exactly the people to whom and with whom leaders need to listen and engage in order to deliver more detailed, workable and improved solutions.

One challenge in embracing resistance is that its first layer often shares the same form of generic, stock phrases, such as:
- We've tried that and it didn't work.
- It may have worked elsewhere but it won't work here.
- It sounds good, but it won't work in practice.

It is important not to accept such stock phrases at this level, but to gently probe and engage in discussion to help people investigate their underlying reasoning. Only if people prove unwilling to examine their objection, or keep changing it, might this suggest underlying, unhealthy resistance. This may be rooted in personal prejudices or agendas which may never be volunteered or overcome. In my experience, though, it is more common that gentle investigations do uncover past lessons or concerns that need to be addressed. Or they may surface wrongly held beliefs or fears about the proposed changes, which can then be eased with more information and assurance.

30. FEAR OF CHANGE

"Don't be afraid; just believe."
(Mark 5v36)

Jesus' exhortations for people to put their faith in him were often accompanied by the encouragement to overcome the fear that he saw in them. Fears are naturally stoked by the prospect of change, but it grieves me if these appear to be packed away in an unexplored state. This can appear to be the case when a friend or colleague asks me about my faith but then shuts the conversation down. Occasionally one of the following responses has been voiced before the conversation is moved on:
- Well, I tried Christianity and it didn't work.
- It's great that it worked for you, but I don't think it would work for me.

My hope is that anyone who finds themselves inclined to similar reactions will consider gently and honestly probing further to reveal any underlying concerns or personal fears – perhaps with a trusted friend. There may not always be an answer to a specific question, but I genuinely believe it is in everyone's best interest to put their faith in Jesus. I therefore trust, and I have seen, that wrongly held beliefs or fears can be surfaced, and/or that more information or assurances are available. In fact, I also commend inviting Father God – if he is indeed real – to help in this gentle probing. Furthermore, I believe he is uniquely able and ready to address fears associated with change, because, as I unexpectedly encountered, his "perfect love drives out fear" (1 John 4v18).

31. Capacity

"We can get loads more out of our current processes – I doubt we've come anywhere close to filling our capacity." (Chapter 7)

Some of the most enjoyable transformations I have facilitated have been in high-growth industries. It is a pleasure to work in a facility where order books are full and the future for the workforce already looks bright. It is also relatively straightforward to make a massive impact quickly, by liberating "hidden capacity" from existing processes. This creates room for extra sales, even from facilities that were thought to be operating flat out. An exponential increase in profit can result, since extra revenue is secured without increasing overhead costs and often without adding labour.

The starting point is to understand the facility's current capacity. The first layer of complexity is that in all but the simplest of facilities, this will depend on product mix (because some products will take longer in some processes than others.) But even when a typical product mix is assumed, estimates for the maximum units that can be produced in a week will vary. These normally reflect how much the facility has managed to produce *in the past*, and they will depend on whether a good week or the best week is assumed. Working with managers, planners, engineers and operators, we then leave historical figures to one side and calculate the facility's potential capacity bottom-up. This is based on a hypothesis of targeted improvement at critical processes and how the facility can be reconfigured and rescheduled. The capacity target we propose is always higher than the facility's weekly record. People have differing degrees of confidence that this can be achieved, which adds to the excitement during implementation as production records are broken week after week. In this scenario a sign of a good transformation is when the whole workforce looks back and wonders how they could ever have been satisfied with anything less.

31. CAPACITY

"I have come that they may have life, and have it to the full."
(John 10v10)

Jesus declared that his mission was to help people have life "to the full". But how much can we expect to get out of life? What does "full" look like?

Perhaps the first thing to acknowledge is that fullness of life might look different to everyone, given our differences. However, it seems there is a consensus today that a full life is one that integrates multiple components. These include physical, mental, emotional, relational and spiritual factors. It may be that you already feel fulfilled: but what if this is just your own "personal best", and more is possible?

I used to have some sort of idea of what it meant to be fulfilled, but after a while this no longer seemed enough. It was during my search for *more* that a hidden, extra dimension unexpectedly opened up and my capacity for life was expanded. I can't necessarily say that I have always felt *happier*, as thankfully I don't think I ever felt particularly *un*happy. Some of the things that make me happy have also changed, and I imagine part of this has resulted from the normal process of growing older – and hopefully wiser! What I do have is a deep-seated joy, something I can best describe as a *surging peace* and a sense of progress as I discover more about Father God and as I become more of the person I believe he has designed me to become. My own adventure towards "full" continues, but I trust I glimpsed a vision of what this might look like in my transforming encounter when my heart was filled to bursting with love.

I hope these *Reflections* might also inspire, challenge and encourage you in your own pursuit of this life in all fullness, which Jesus offers to us all.

www.ingramcontent.com/pod-product-compliance
Lightning Source LLC
Chambersburg PA
CBHW052135010526
44113CB00036B/2266